BUREAUCRACY AND FOREIGN POLICY

Studies in International Affairs Number 17

BUREAUCRACY AND FOREIGN POLICY

by Francis E. Rourke

58367

The Washington Center of Foreign Policy Research
School of Advanced International Studies
The Johns Hopkins University

The Johns Hopkins University Press,
Baltimore and London

The Johns Hopkins University Press, Baltimore, Md. 21218
The Johns Hopkins University Press Ltd., London

Library of Congress Catalog Card Number 73–186516

ISBN 0–8018–1394–8 (clothbound edition)
ISBN 0–8018–1399–9 (paperbound edition)

Originally published, 1972
Paperbound edition, 1972

Library of Congress Cataloging in Publication data
will be found on the last printed page of this book.

FOREWORD

In a period of the apparent retrenchment of America's external involvements analysts naturally become more conscious of the domestic determinants of foreign policy. In the Washington Center of Foreign Policy's continuing examination of the changing international and domestic environment of American foreign policy Professor Francis E. Rourke contributes a special insight into the politics and institutions of the policy process. Going beyond current academic preoccupation with the constraints imposed by bureaucratic politics, public opinion, and Congress, he examines the basic structure of power within which the president now, as heretofore, so largely shapes foreign policy. A further development of his interpretation of the domestic context of American policy will appear in 1973 in the forthcoming sequel to the Center's first quadrennial volume of *America and the World,* to which he also contributed a chapter.

ROBERT E. OSGOOD
Director
Washington Center of
Foreign Policy Research

In recent years bureaucratic organizations have come to be regarded as major centers of decision in foreign affairs. A theory of bureaucratic determinism has emerged which credits executive agencies with virtually total control over the development of American policy abroad. A decade or so ago explanations of American foreign policy stressed the significance of tidal shifts of public opinion, or what was then called the "mood" of the electorate. Now the force of public opinion in international affairs is discounted, and it is the bureaucratic apparatus which is at the center of attention.

Clearly, executive agencies play an increasingly important role in foreign policy. But they are still far from being as preeminent as some commentators have assumed. The political stakes of presidents and their personal perspectives on foreign affairs are more decisive than any other factors shaping the character of American involvement abroad. The conduct of foreign policy under President Nixon and the dominant position of his special assistant for national security affairs, Henry Kissinger, provide dramatic evidence of this fact on the contemporary scene.

Thus, foreign policy today is the product of a system of executive decision-making in which the president and his political appointees play a leading role and career bureaucrats are often relegated to minor parts. If fundamental reform of the foreign policy process is sought, it will be found not in administrative reorganization but through a reordering of the basic political structure which will have the effect of limiting what is now virtually a presidential monopoly over the conduct of foreign policy.

I am very appreciative of the kindness of colleagues and friends who read this essay and made many suggestions toward its improvement: Matthew Crenson, Virginia Ermer, Maggie Gaines, Paul Schulman, and Robert W. Tucker. The manuscript was prepared for publication by Evelyn Scheulen— a skilled typist and a warm friend.

CONTENTS

BUREAUCRACY AND FOREIGN POLICY

Studies in International Affairs Number 17

I. DECISION-MAKING IN FOREIGN AFFAIRS

For much of the period between World Wars I and II concern over the conduct of foreign policy in the United States focused upon the question of whether executive officials would be able to rally public support for policies that developments abroad required the United States to pursue. The greatest threat to a foreign policy rationally designed to further the national interest was thus seen as coming from the American people, in the form of either indifference to policies that executive officials considered necessary or pressure for policies that these officials knew were unwise. In this traditional image of the foreign policy process the executive role was identified with rationality while public participation in decision-making was regarded as a source of irrationality in foreign affairs.

The irrationality of the electorate was commonly seen as stemming from its fickleness—a tendency toward radical and unpredictable shifts in the attitudes of the American people on the role of the United States in world politics. From this perspective the conduct of American foreign policy had an unhealthy dependence upon the "mood" of the American public, with every prospect that a sudden alteration in public sentiment might drastically curtail the options open to policy-makers. Gabriel Almond, for example, suggested in 1950 that the American public has a tendency to over-react in a bellicose way to what it perceives as threats from abroad and to be lulled into a false sense of security by the appearance of serenity on the international scene.[1]

In a celebrated critique of the role of public opinion in the foreign policy process, Walter Lippmann extended this indictment to all the Western democracies. The people have acquired devastating power over foreign policy in modern democratic societies, he contended. "They have compelled the governments, which usually knew what would have been wiser, or was necessary or was more expedient, to be too late with too little, or too long with too much, too pacifist in peace and too bellicose in war, too neutralist or appeasing in negotiation or too intransigent. Mass opinion has . . . shown itself to be a dangerous master of decision when the stakes are life and death."[2] Lippmann is highly critical of both the ignorance and the inertia of mass opinion— arguing that public awareness of what is happening in international politics always lags far behind the vision of responsible officials in the executive branch.

However, in the twenty-year period following World War II it became increasingly clear that public attitudes did not seriously limit the foreign policy decisions of executive officials. Quite to the contrary the public exhibited a growing disposition to accord these officials wide latitude in foreign policy decisions and, when it was required, gave strong

[1] Gabriel A. Almond, *The American People and Foreign Policy* (New York: Harcourt, Brace, 1950), pp. 54–55. For a recent appraisal of the Almond thesis, see William R. Caspary, "The 'Mood Theory': A Study of Public Opinion and Foreign Policy," *American Political Science Review* 64 (June 1970): 536–47.

[2] Walter Lippmann, *The Public Philosophy* (New York: Mentor Books, 1956), p. 24.

backing to American activities abroad in the years between 1945 and 1965. Moreover, during this Cold War era executive agencies themselves acquired a formidable ability to mold public attitudes toward foreign affairs. Whatever their other effects, these developments made it extremely difficult to regard the public as having a significant capacity to direct foreign policy down paths of irrational behavior.

Indeed, after the beginning in 1965 of the massive American involvement in Vietnam, the question that increasingly came to the fore in discussions of the foreign policy process was whether public opinion could hope to affect decision-making in foreign affairs at all. There was a growing belief that decisions in this area were made entirely at the discretion of the executive branch, except on those occasions when policy decisions might impose highly visible and substantial burdens on the electorate, such as higher taxes or expanded draft calls. In his attacks upon American policy in Vietnam in the 1960s, Lippmann was confronted by the embarrassing fact that the irrationality he condemned was the product, not of the power of public opinion, but of an executive branch he had once pictured as the only source of intelligent decisions in foreign affairs.

The Specter of Bureaucracy

As fears of the harmful effect of public opinion upon decision-making in foreign affairs have receded, a new problem has come to the fore in American politics—the role and power of executive organizations in the foreign policy process. Increasingly in recent years, these organizations have come to be looked upon as having the capacity to influence policy in ways no less irrational than those once attributed to public opinion. It is, for example, now argued that bureaucracies push for policies designed to serve not so much the national interest as their own hegemonial ambitions as organizations—competing more for primacy in the governmental structure of the United States than with any foreign adversary.

Some of the criticism of the bureaucratic role in the foreign policy process that has been made in recent years has been a form of scapegoating. Since 1965 the trauma of Vietnam has led to a continuing search for villains upon whom the blame for American intervention in Southeast Asia can be fixed, and the search has led as often as not to bureaucratic organizations in foreign affairs as the chief culprits. There are other villains of course. Presidential ego is often singled out for special notice—the reluctance of President Lyndon Johnson, for example, to be "the first American President to lose a war."[3]

Clearly, presidents have a substantial ego investment in the success of their foreign policies, since the longevity of a president's political career as well as his place in history often depends upon his success in foreign affairs. While it is difficult to disentangle the influence of this factor from the other elements involved in foreign policy decisions, there is considerable evidence that it has been substantial in the case of all three of the most recent presidents—Kennedy, Johnson, and Nixon. It has not always been clear whether the "humiliation" these presi-

[3] See, in this connection, Townsend Hoopes, *The Limits of Intervention* (New York: David McKay Co., 1969), pp. 113–16, 181, 240; and George Reedy, *The Twilight of the Presidency* (New York: The World Publishing Co., 1970).

dents have worried about in their discussions of Vietnam has been personal or national.

But more often than not, the attempt to fix responsibility for the failures of Vietnam has led to the bureaucratic apparatus. Former members of the Kennedy administration have led the way in attacks on the role of bureaucracy in foreign affairs—in part perhaps in an effort to shift the blame for Vietnam from the political echelons in which they had temporarily served to the career bureaucrats they had always held in some contempt.

In an essay entitled "How to Control the Military" John Kenneth Galbraith explains the American involvement in the Vietnam War in the following terms:

> It was the result of a long series of steps taken in response to a bureaucratic view of the world— a view to which a President willingly or unwillingly yielded and which, until much too late, was unchecked by any legislative or public opposition. This view was of a planet threatened by an imminent takeover by the unified and masterful forces of the Communist world, directed from Moscow (or later and with less assurance from Peking) and coming to a focus, however improbably, some thousands of miles away in the activities of a few thousand guerrillas against the markedly regressive government of South Vietnam.[4]

Nowhere does Galbraith indicate why this is a particularly "bureaucratic view of the world" rather

[4] John Kenneth Galbraith, *How to Control the Military* (New York: Signet Books, 1969), pp 16–17.

than the standard anti-Communist posture that had long been a staple commodity of American politics, shared and disseminated by all the principal agencies of opinion in the society. Indeed, rather than originating or necessarily sharing in this conventional anti-Communist ideology, many bureaucrats had been its victim—eliminated from government service in the 1950s because of their alleged association with subversive activity.

This antibureaucratic animus has also been very prominent in the work of another former member of the Kennedy administration, Arthur M. Schlesinger, Jr. Since his departure from the government, Schlesinger has been highly critical of the national security bureaucracy for failures of a negative character, such as the reluctance of the State Department to implement innovative proposals by President Kennedy for détente with the Soviet Union, as well as for those of a more positive nature, like the erroneous information given Kennedy by the CIA at the time of his disastrous decision to support an invasion of Cuba at the Bay of Pigs in 1961.[5]

Criticism of bureaucracy can thus serve the same function in the United States that it has in the Soviet Union—as a device by which blame for failures in policy can be shifted from political to administrative elites—from a party that can do no wrong to a bureaucracy that is often made to seem as though it can do no right. In both countries politicians may abandon policies they have sponsored once it is clear that these programs are not going to be successful. A bureaucratic organization charged with responsi-

[5] See Arthur M. Schlesinger, Jr., *A Thousand Days* (Boston: Houghton Mifflin Co., 1965).

bility for administering such orphaned policies may even find itself under savage attack by these erstwhile parents for the care it is giving their offspring. In some ways this has been the fate of American military organizations in Vietnam, which after 1968 were left with the thankless task of carrying on a war in Southeast Asia from which its political sponsors at home were largely trying to disassociate themselves.

The critical attitude of liberals like Galbraith and Schlesinger toward the role of bureaucracy in the conduct of foreign policy stands in stark contrast to the support American liberalism has traditionally given to the activities of bureaucrats in the domestic sector of American politics. Liberals have traditionally looked upon executive agencies as instruments for the achievement of humane and progressive values within American society—providing welfare and other services for underprivileged groups and protecting the public through the regulatory process from predatory economic practices by powerful industrial firms. (This support has weakened in recent years, as bureaucratic organizations have come under heavy fire for failing to achieve the domestic goals for which they were created.)

Until recently, conservatives were the chief critics of the growing power of bureaucracy in the American political system; they are still very hostile toward many of the domestic activities of executive agencies, especially welfare and antipoverty programs. In the sphere of foreign affairs, however, the attachment of conservatives to the military has tended to mute their criticism of bureaucracy, since the military component of the national security apparatus is so large. Even cost overruns in defense procurement operations have failed to arouse the customary conservative wrath against evidence of waste and inefficiency in bureaucracy. Of course, conservative hostility toward executive organizations still surfaces periodically in this area of policy. In 1970 when the Coast Guard forced a defecting Russian seaman to return to his ship, there were bitter attacks by conservatives upon bureaucratic bungling in foreign affairs. But in the main it is correct to say that the threat of bureaucratic power in foreign policy is a specter that primarily haunts liberal thought in modern American politics.

Assessing Bureaucratic Power

While the power of bureaucratic organizations over decisions in foreign affairs has sometimes been exaggerated for political reasons, it is clear that these organizations have come to play a tremendously important role in the foreign policy process since World War II. American involvement in world affairs and the onset of the Cold War after 1945 brought a swift increase in the number and size of the executive agencies engaged in the administration of foreign affairs and put billions of dollars at the disposal of the national security apparatus in the United States. Because of these developments, it was inevitable that the foreign policy process in this country would be "bureaucratized." As new executive organizations have been created and old organizations expanded to handle foreign policy problems, career officials have acquired expanding influence in making and carrying out decisions.

It was observed in the previous section that administrative agencies are sometimes blamed for failures in policies they have not initiated. But it should also be noted that these organizations are not entirely innocent bystanders in situations of this kind. Executive agencies may enthusiastically pursue policies that are clearly ineffectual from the point of view of the national welfare, simply because these programs continue to serve the interests of the organizations themselves. As a result they may stand in the way of efforts to liquidate unprofitable activities in the sphere of foreign affairs. Thus, in the case of Vietnam the armed forces did not originate the policies that brought on the American commitment to that part of the world. But once military organizations were committed to combat in a massive way, they acquired substantial interests of their own in the war—their institutional pride was involved in the success of an effort they were largely responsible for carrying on, they received much larger appropriations and they acquired combat experience as well as opportunities for career advancement.

War may not always be, as Randolph Bourne once argued, "the health of the state." In some societies it has brought the destruction of the state, and the costs of Vietnam in terms of domestic disorder and the erosion of state authority have been very substantial in the United States. But war may well be a tonic for state organizations charged with responsibility for waging it, and the goals of these organizations may lead them to pursue it even when it has disastrous consequences for the welfare of their own nation.

The purpose of this inquiry is to examine the kinds

of power that bureaucratic organizations exert in the area of foreign policy—the sources from which such influence is derived and the channels through which it shapes governmental actions. Our major goal is to put this power into proper perspective—to ascertain the full range of possibilities for exercising influence that bureaucratic organizations possess, and yet to see also the limits or boundaries of this power.

It should be noted at the outset that the foreign affairs bureaucracy with which we are concerned is a family of organizations, whose members are linked together but nevertheless retain an independent life of their own. The kinds of bureaucratic influence described in the following pages are not equally shared by all members of this interorganizational network. While the years since World War II have seen a substantial rise in the fortunes of the Department of Defense, they have also witnessed a marked decline in the organizational stature of the State Department. This diversity of experience has to be kept in mind in appraising the accuracy of all generalizations about the role of bureaucracy in foreign policy.

But it remains true that each executive agency is far from being an autonomous agent in making policy decisions. There are many areas of policy in which agencies share power with each other in such a way that the precise role of each organization is difficult to identify. Such interrelationships may be quite informal or may take place under formal institutional auspices, such as the National Security Council. Moreover, they may result in either an expansion or a contraction of an organization's influence. According to studies conducted by the Senate Subcommittee on National Policy-Making, such interorganizational participation in decision-making has led to an increase in the influence of the Treasury Department and a corresponding decline in the role of the State Department in foreign affairs.

Interaction with Private Organizations

The influence of executive agencies on decision-making is also greatly affected by patterns of interaction with organizations outside the government. Indeed, some critics of bureaucracy on the left have argued that executive agencies are nothing more than the pawns of the powerful economic organizations in American society with which they deal. Gabriel Kolko discounts the importance of the executive apparatus in foreign affairs altogether. "These bureaucratic structures," he writes, "are less the source of power than the means by which others direct power in America for predetermined purposes." [6] Basic to Kolko's conception of foreign policy is his belief that "bureaucrats do not represent their own tangible interests . . . for behind the bureaucrats exist levels of economic and political power, whether latent or exercised . . . . It is this ultimate power that defines the limits of bureaucratic conduct and the functions of the state." [7] Given this commitment to economic determinism, it is inevitable that Kolko will regard executive agencies as playing

[6] Gabriel Kolko, *The Roots of American Foreign Policy* (Boston: The Beacon Press, 1969), p. 4. Much the same view is taken by G. William Dumhoff, *Who Rules America?* (Englewood Cliffs, New Jersey: Prentice Hall, 1967), pp. 115–31.

[7] *Ibid.,* pp. 4–5.

11

a secondary role in foreign affairs. "At every level of the administration of the American state, domestically and internationally, business serves as the fount of critical assumptions or goals and strategically placed personnel . . . one can only assess the other institutional structures . . . in relation to the predominance of the economic ruling class." [8]

Kolko directs particular fire at the notion that the military bureaucracy plays an important role in the development of foreign policy in the United States. He argues that "the military is a most conformist and pliable aspect of the power system, quite drably bureaucratic, and it serves the purposes of capitalists and politicians without much reticence. . . . It has dissented no more than any other group of bureaucrats serving the state." [9] This suggestion that the failure of the military to dissent from the main outlines of American foreign policy signifies its subordinate role in decision-making is highly questionable. It is no less plausible to assume that the absence of such dissent indicates the degree to which foreign policy already conforms to the preferences of the military.

The conception of the foreign affairs bureaucracy as simply the tool of powerful private economic organizations is by no means a universal position on the left. Some writers of this political persuasion, such as C. Wright Mills, have tended to regard the military bureaucracy as being in some sense a "power elite," exercising a great deal of control over foreign policy decisions. [10] It is very common in the literature

[8] *Ibid.,* p. 26.

[9] *Ibid.,* pp. 33–34, 37.

[10] See C. Wright Mills, *The Power Elite* (New York: Oxford University Press, 1956).

on the left, for example, for organizations like the State Department, the CIA, and the Pentagon to be credited with playing a major role in the suppression of revolutionary movements abroad.

A compromise interpretation is offered by Richard J. Barnet. He argues that foreign policy is made by a group of "national security managers" who move freely from executive positions in private business organizations into high governmental office and use both vantage points to shape decisions. While the decisions of national security managers are tailored to fit the needs of the dominant economic interests of American society, they must control the bureaucratic apparatus in order to make them.[11]

Obviously, there are many illustrations of foreign policy decisions in which bureaucrats seem to be acting as agents of private economic interests, such as the representations made by U.S. embassy officials in Latin America in behalf of firms whose property is threatened with expropriation. But on equally frequent occasions private business organizations make or reverse decisions on investments abroad at the request of government agencies, as, for example, when such firms pass up opportunities for profitable investment in iron curtain countries under pressure from the State Department. Thus, while the foreign affairs bureaucracy reflects patterns of economic power within the United States, it also has an impressive capacity to shape the decisions of business and industrial organizations.

[11] For a summary of Barnet's views, see Richard M. Pfeffer, ed., *No More Vietnams?* (New York: Harper & Row, 1968), pp. 50–74.

Bureaucrats and Politicians

Ultimately, however, the most important "outside" groups with which executive agencies share power are the political institutions to which they are linked in the American governmental system. Policies established in organizations like political parties and legislative committees set boundaries beyond which it is perilous for bureaucratic decision-making to stray. In the 1950s, for example, hostility toward the Communist Chinese in these political centers made it mandatory for the State Department to oppose and organize international resistance against the seating of the Peking regime in the United Nations. The boundaries established in these institutions are ill-defined in some places and weakly defended in others, but they nevertheless represent barriers which bureaucrats cannot altogether ignore in their own deliberations.

Foremost of all the political institutions which bureaucratic organizations must take into account in making decisions is the office of the president, whose involvement in foreign policy has been a dominant factor in the evolution of American politics over the past two decades. From the point of view of public policy, foreign affairs is clearly the most critical area of presidential responsibility. In the first place, the constitution assigns this task to him—witness the provisions giving the president power to appoint ambassadors and making him commander-in-chief of the armed forces. But even in the absence of such explicit constitutional requirements, presidents would inevitably give foreign policy the highest priority of attention in view of the catastrophic consequences international conflict could have in an age of nuclear weapons.

Considerations of political advantage also lead presidents to give primacy to foreign affairs. In the international area the president enjoys an initiative and an autonomy that he lacks in domestic policy, where he must commonly bargain with Congress or private groups to achieve his objectives. Presidents can thus assist their own political careers as well as the fortunes of the political party over which they preside by focusing the political agenda upon issues of foreign policy. Here the public is likely to side with the president, and Congress is prone to defer to his leadership. The chief executive can therefore more easily emerge with a record of successful achievement that he can convert into political victory on election day. "Since World War II," Aaron Wildavsky writes, "Presidents have had much greater success in controlling the nation's defense and foreign policies than in dominating its domestic policies."[12] Thus foreign policy is not an area in which bureaucratic organizations can carve power out of presidential indifference, as is sometimes the case in other areas of policy.

The pages that follow examine the various sources in which bureaucratic influence over foreign affairs is rooted. This preliminary discussion has emphasized the fact that bureaucrats do not wield an exclusive or monopolistic kind of authority in foreign affairs. They exercise influence in an environment in which a variety of other participants also have power over policy decisions. Some of these

[12] Aaron Wildavsky, "The Two Presidencies," *Trans-Action* 4 (December 1966): 7.

participants are outside of government—defense industries, for example, or business firms with substantial investments abroad. Others, like the presidency, are at the apex of a political system in which bureaucrats occupy—in law at least—subordinate positions. Ascertaining the precise degree of influence which administrative officials have in such a plural universe of power is not easy.

The task is further complicated by the fact that the share of influence held by bureaucratic organizations may be highly unstable. As the history of the Vietnam War reveals, the influence of executive agencies may quickly erode if the policies they are carrying out require substantial sacrifices on the part of the public or jeopardize the election prospects of officeholders. For bureaucratic influence in the policy process to flourish, public opinion must remain quiescent, and the security of elected officials must not be threatened. However, the necessity of maintaining such public quiescence and of assuring the political safety of officeholders is itself a formidable restraint upon the power of bureaucratic organizations in foreign affairs.

We thus reject the notion of "bureaucratic determinism"—the theory that foreign policy in the United States is entirely the product of self-serving machinations by executive organizations. It must be conceded, however, that American foreign policy in recent years can hardly be explained without reference to the drives and characteristics of the institutions responsible for carrying it out. The Cold War has provided a fertile setting for the realization of imperialist ambitions on the part of bureaucratic organizations as well as nations, since these organizations also have hegemonial goals. Indeed, on frequent occasions executive agencies have appeared to regard competition with the Communist powers as a heaven-sent opportunity to make the world safe for American bureaucracy.

II. BUREAUCRATIC COMMUNICATIONS

A fundamental source of bureaucratic power in foreign affairs is the ability of career officials to mold the views of other participants in the foreign policy process. Bureaucratic organizations are as much as anything else information systems, and the data they analyze and transmit cannot help but influence the way events outside the United States are perceived by others. This information may be in the form of reports on what is actually happening in remote parts of the world like the Tonkin Gulf. Executive agencies may also interpret the meaning of these events for the United States or suggest an appropriate response by the American government in the light of what is alleged to have occurred.

There are two major audiences for such bureaucratic communications on foreign affairs. Of critical importance are the political elites within government, particularly in the White House, who bear responsibility for initiating policy decisions or—in the case of Congress—providing the resources necessary for carrying these decisions out. A second target is the varied groups outside the governmental apparatus which have the ability to influence the conduct of foreign policy.

This latter category includes the mass public, whose views as mirrored in public opinion polls can affect the durability of policy, as well as the "attentive" groups, who take a continuing interest in foreign affairs and whose activities can, as agitation over the Vietnam War demonstrated, affect the capacity of the government for effective action overseas. It also embraces the media of communication, which transmit information from governmental and nongovernmental sources to the public, and may on frequent occasions shape the meaning of information in the process of supplying it.

While the efforts of executive agencies to frame the opinions of officeholders and outside publics can be separated for purposes of analysis, these activities are very closely related in practice. When bureaucratic organizations are successful in forming the attitudes of political elites within government, they can anticipate help from these officials in sustaining public support for executive decisions and programs. Conversely, opposition from political officeholders will very often trigger dissent among outside groups which look to these officials for guidance on policy issues.

In the same way, the views of officeholders tend to mirror the opinions of their constituents. In the case of the great public debate over Vietnam, for example, congressional critics of the war were emboldened in their opposition by the activities of peace groups outside of government. During those periods when executive officials were able to still this outside dissent by managing to keep the appearance or the reality of activities in the war zone at a low level, they were also able to diminish the vigor of congressional criticism.

Political Elites

The process by which bureaucrats shape the perspectives of political officeholders in government has been given various names, from "brainwashing" in colloquial language to "socialization" as it is sometimes described in academic literature. Whatever term is used, the phenomenon it designates is the capacity of bureaucrats to determine at least the premises on which political elites make judgments on issues of public policy. It was Herbert Simon who first drew attention to the utility of being able to shape the value or factual premises of decision-makers as a means of insuring control over decisions themselves.[1]

In the case of foreign policy, it is clear that bu-reaucratic and political officials do not ordinarily differ in their basic value premise—the importance of advancing the security interests of the United States and protecting those interests from hostile actions by foreign powers. What bureaucrats can do, however, is induce political officials to rank na-tional security issues much higher on their agenda of concern than might otherwise be the case by altering the factual premises upon which policy-makers are operating. They can, for example, draw attention to what they regard as threats to American security interests of which policy-makers may not be aware and suggest ways and means of dealing with such threats, or in the absence of immediate problems, they can propose measures designed to prevent the emergence of future crises.

A notable illustration of the bureaucratic role in this regard was the influence exerted by George Kennan from his vantage point in the State Depart-ment in the years immediately following World War II. During this period, Kennan's arguments on the need to contain Soviet power and the methods by which this goal might be achieved did much to shape

[1] Herbert Simon, *Administrative Behavior*, 2nd ed. (New York: The Macmillan Co., 1957).

the basic assumptions on which American foreign policy was based in dealing with the Communist powers around the world. The views expressed in his celebrated article in *Foreign Affairs* became the basic American text of the Cold War for both government officials and attentive publics outside of government.[2]

The influence that bureaucrats exert on the policy process through their power to give advice should not be exaggerated. The Cold War experience suggests that it is easiest for bureaucrats to appear powerful when their advice matches and reinforces the pre-existing views of the political officials responsible for policy. As noted above, the advice of Kennan seemed highly influential in the early days of the Cold War, when the doctrine of containment was eminently congenial to the goals of leading political elites in the country. Later on, however, when Kennan attempted to restrain policy-makers from putting undue emphasis upon military force in applying the principle of containment, his advice was largely ignored, and he found himself increasingly isolated from power.[3] Hence, the best way for a bureaucrat to acquire a reputation as an *éminence grise* may be to confine himself to advice that fits in with the views of his political superiors, or to give advice only in areas in which he knows his superior has no strong opinions. Even so powerful a bureaucrat as the president's special assistant for national

[2] George F. Kennan, "The Sources of Soviet Conduct," *Foreign Affairs* 25 (July 1947): 566–82.

[3] For an account of this rise and fall in one bureaucrat's influence, see George F. Kennan, *Memoirs 1925–1950* (Boston: Little, Brown and Co., 1967), esp. pp. 354–67.

security affairs is subject to some of the same limitations in this respect as an ordinary career bureaucrat.

For example, the special assistant for national security affairs under President Nixon, Henry Kissinger, enjoys a wide reputation as a strong and influential advisor of the president in contemporary American politics. Both the secretary of state and the secretary of defense are generally regarded as ranking far behind Kissinger in the extent to which they influence presidential decisions. Alone among all high officials in the foreign policy establishment, Kissinger is protected by the doctrine of executive privilege from having to appear for questioning before Congress, and with close proximity to the president, he does not have to surmount the formidable bureaucratic obstacles that a State Department official would confront in trying to get his views before the chief executive. Yet it is a fair assumption that Nixon initially chose Kissinger for his position because his views generally coincided with Nixon's own orientation toward foreign policy. Moreover, Kissinger's role in office may sometimes be that of reinforcing Nixon's capacity to pursue policies of his own choice, serving as an advocate or defender of the president's policies with the National Security Council and the other executive agencies charged with responsibility for foreign affairs.

But while it is necessary to recognize that the appearance and reality of bureaucratic power may not always coincide, it cannot be denied that the ability of bureaucrats to channel information into policy deliberations provides substantial leverage with which to affect the shape of decisions. If there are cases in which bureaucrats appear only to be telling political officials what they want to hear, there are equally striking illustrations of situations in which staff members of executive agencies have substantially reshaped the views of political leaders in both Congress and the executive. A notable example in this regard is the shift in the views of Clark Clifford on the Vietnam War following his appointment as Secretary of Defense in 1968—a change that occurred in good part as a result of briefings Clifford received from his civilian staff after he took over at the Pentagon.[4]

Bureaucratic advice is most compelling in its impact on policy decisions when it approaches unanimity in viewpoint. Hence, the traditional safeguard against the aggrandizement of bureaucratic power through advisory channels has been the assumption that administrative officials and organizations will disagree on foreign policy questions and that this disagreement will give the public and its elected officials an opportunity to choose among alternative lines of advice from the executive apparatus.

In an article written in 1961 Samuel P. Huntington suggested that differences in viewpoint among military organizations expanded the president's freedom of choice in foreign policy by giving him many more options to choose from. In the days before real unification of the armed forces had occurred, the president could always find some military support for whatever course of action he decided upon. The military organizations never presented a united front

[4] See Townsend Hoopes, *The Limits of Intervention* (New York: David McKay Co., 1969), pp. 151–224.

which he might find politically difficult if not impossible to oppose.[5]

But recent history suggests that these organizations disagree much less frequently on issues of national security policy than might be expected. More commonly they contend for primacy in carrying out policy decisions, or for hegemony over new weapons systems and national security missions. The rivalry among the army, the air force and the navy for control over roles and missions in the Cold War is legendary. Boundary disputes among these organizations have produced conflict almost as intense as the struggle between the United States and the Soviet Union in international politics.[6]

Interorganizational competition of this sort over jurisdictional matters is not the same as debate over issues of substantive policy. Here a consensus often develops which binds all bureaucratic organizations together as to what policies the security interests of the United States require. When such a consensus emerges, it greatly increases the influence of bureaucratic advice upon presidential decision-making in foreign affairs. Consider, for example, the situation faced by President Johnson in his first year in office:

In the summer of 1964 the President instructed his chief advisers to prepare for him as wide a

[5] See Samuel P. Huntington, "Interservice Competition and the Political Roles of the Armed Services," *American Political Science Review* 55 (March 1961): 40–52, and *The Common Defense* (New York: Columbia University Press, 1961), pp. 369–425.

[6] For a recent discussion of such interorganizational rivalries and their effect upon national security policy-making, see Morton H. Halperin, "Why Bureaucrats Play Games," *Foreign Policy,* Spring 1971, pp. 70–90.

range of Vietnam options as possible for post-election consideration and decision. He explicitly asked that all options be laid out. What happened next was, in effect, Lyndon Johnson's slow-motion Bay of Pigs. For the advisers so effectively converged on one single option—juxtaposed against two other, phony options (in effect, blowing up the world, or scuttle-and-run)—that the President was confronted with unanimity for bombing the North from all his trusted counselors.[7]

Moreover, even where such a consensus does not exist, certain factors tend to prevent differences of opinion among executive officials from impairing the appearance of unanimity in the advice emanating from the bureaucratic apparatus in foreign affairs. Authority in bureaucratic structures is usually distributed in a hierarchical fashion, making it impolitic for subordinates to disagree openly with superior officials who control job assignments, promotional opportunities and other avenues of career advancement. In all executive agencies the tendency rather has been for dissenters to suppress their misgivings and to go along with what appears to be an organizational consensus.

The structuring of organizations along hierarchical lines is by no means the only factor helping to maintain the unity and hence the impact of bureaucratic advice in foreign affairs. James Thomson has called attention to the "curator mentality" which prevails in the Department of State—a career orientation which makes the preservation of past policy

[7] James C. Thomson, Jr., "How Could Vietnam Happen? An Autopsy," *The Atlantic* 221 (April 1968): 52.

the primary responsibility of the bureaucrat rather than the initiation of new ideas.[8] Others, like John Harr and Andrew Scott, have noted the department's inhospitable attitude toward the research and intelligence functions—activities that might be institutional wellsprings of innovation and dissent.[9]

There is also an element of risk involved in dissent which helps to maintain unanimity within bureaucratic organizations. The bureaucratic consensus that emerged in the 1950s over the need to isolate and contain Communist China was prompted in no small measure by collective memories of the penalties visited upon American officials whose advice was regarded as somehow responsible for the fall of China to communism after World War II.

As suggested earlier, the organizational vantage point from which bureaucratic advice can most readily influence presidential decisions is the office of the special assistant for national security affairs. This office enjoys an advantage over other bureaucratic organizations in the field of foreign affairs because it has no constituency other than the president himself. Indeed it was created for precisely the purpose of providing the president with assistance in framing national security policy from an organization that had no function other than that of serving him, no allies in Congress, and no bureaucratic interests or identity of its own to advance or protect.

Ironically, however, an office which was designed

[8] *Ibid.*, p. 50.

[9] John E. Harr, *The Professional Diplomat* (Princeton: Princeton University Press, 1969), pp. 124–27; Andrew M. Scott, "Environmental Change and Organizational Adaptation: The Problem of the State Department," *International Studies Quarterly* 13 (March 1970): 85–94.

in large part to protect the president from becoming the prisoner of bureaucratic advice has itself acquired substantial influence over his decisions. In part this is because the office serves as a conduit through which information from other bureaucratic organizations is channeled to the president, and in part it is because the office has acquired formidable advisory power of its own. It has already been suggested that the national security adviser, like the other courtiers of the president, must often play the tunes that he knows his sovereign likes to hear. But any official sitting astride the channels of communication to the White House is in a strong position to control what the president does in fact hear.

Bureaucratic organizations in the defense establishment devote much of their advisory efforts to shaping the views of political elites in Congress rather than the executive, and their activity in this respect has met with considerable success. Secretary of Defense Melvin Laird recently boasted that the department had not lost a single vote in Congress during the two and one-half years he had been in office. The House and Senate Armed Services Committees provide perhaps as good examples as exist of congressmen whose views have been shaped by the executive agencies with which they deal.

In general, however, it is fair to say that the efforts of executive agencies to mold the attitudes of political elites in Congress are mainly directed at advancing their own organizational interests, such as larger appropriations, improved wage scales, or expanded jurisdiction. Efforts to influence substantive foreign policy decisions are more commonly channeled in the direction of the White House—

toward the president and his cadre of political advisers. Of course, when an agency fails in its efforts to win over the president to its point of view on policy questions, it may well turn to Congress in an effort to generate political pressure which will change his mind.

Building Public Support

A large part of the communications activity in which national security agencies engage is addressed, not to political elites within government, but to external audiences—the publics outside of government who concern themselves with foreign policy issues. These agencies recognize that if they are successful in generating a high level of public support for their views on policy questions they increase the likelihood that the proposals they advocate will become official policy and reduce the possibility that the government will adopt programs to which they are opposed. Success in molding public opinion can also give executive agencies a substantial advantage in their continuing efforts to aggrandize their authority at the expense of organizational competitors.

The various members of the family of organizations which make up the bureaucratic apparatus in foreign affairs show a great disparity in their ability to build influence in this way. The most vigorous and effective of all agencies in shaping the contours of public opinion have long been the military organizations. The defense establishment has far larger resources available for carrying on public relations programs designed to win the "minds and hearts" of the American people than do other executive agencies in the network of organizations concerned with foreign affairs. Estimates of the annual expenditures of the Pentagon in the area of public information activity vary widely, but they appear to compare favorably with the amount spent on news programming by the three major television networks in the United States.

A heavily subsidized public relations program is not, however, the only advantage the Defense Department enjoys in its effort to win support from publics outside the government. Quite apart from the power to persuade, the department's strength, in terms of public support, rests upon some very tangible assets in its possession. Through defense expenditures, the Pentagon is able to distribute economic benefits to a wide variety of industries and local communities. Defense budgets long ago eclipsed rivers and harbors appropriations as the major governmental "pork-barrel" nourishing the domestic economy.

The military has been operating for years in that Elysium of the public relations man, a seller's market. Take the climate into which the Sentinel ABM program was introduced. Many people looked on it, as they now look on Safeguard, not as a weapon but as a means of prosperity. For the industrialist it means profits; for the worker new jobs and the prospect of higher wages; for the politician a new installation or defense order with which to ingratiate himself with his constituents. Military expenditures today provide the livelihood of some ten percent of our work force. There are 22,000 major corporate defense contractors and another 100,000 subcontractors. Defense plants or installations are located in 363 of the country's 435 congressional districts. Even before it turns its attention to the public-at-large, the military has a large and sympathetic audience for its message.[10]

In addition to these very tangible assets which enable the defense establishment to function as a source of prosperity for substantial segments of American society, the military role exerts a symbolic appeal that is as rare among bureaucratic organizations in the United States as it is in other societies. The identification of the military with national pride and achievement—in a word, with patriotism—is a quite extraordinary bureaucratic resource—setting the Defense Department apart from all other executive agencies in the country.

Moreover, for a considerable part of the population an identification with the military springs from public as well as nationalistic motives, based as it is upon employment by the department, membership in the National Guard or one of the military reserve units, or status as a veteran of one of the branches of the armed forces. Large numbers of Americans are thus members or former members of the military organizations which seek their support and that of their families through well-financed public relations programs, and they frequently belong to veterans' organizations which indoctrinate them on the virtues of supporting the goals and policies of the military.

Perhaps the best measure we have of the secure

---

[10] Senator J. William Fulbright, *The Pentagon Propaganda Machine* (New York: Vintage Books, 1971), p. 12.

position of the Defense Department in the public eye is the ability it has displayed in recent years to withstand innumerable blows to its prestige—blows that could easily have capsized any ordinary civilian agency of government. These setbacks flow especially from events connected with the Vietnam War, including the atrocities perpetrated against the Vietnamese population (particularly at My Lai), and drug addiction among American troops stationed in Southeast Asia. They also stem from developments outside of Vietnam, such as the surveillance carried on by the military over civilian protest activity in the United States and scandals associated with the army's management of its PX system overseas.

Failures on the part of a civilian agency often reduce it to ignominious status in the view of the public. The failures of military organization can scarcely be admitted, so deeply do they strike at personal as well as organizational pride. A setback in the war on poverty only reflects adversely on the extravagance of the goal or the incompetence of the bureaucratic organizations charged with achieving it. Indeed it only confirms the unfavorable public stereotype of bureaucracy. But to lose an armed conflict with a national adversary is widely regarded as a humiliating blow to every citizen's sense of self-esteem.

Executive organizations in the field of foreign affairs other than the Defense Department are far less fortunately situated with respect to their ability to shape public opinion. Among such agencies only the Peace Corps can be said to have had substantial success in recent years in generating a very favorable public attitude toward itself and its work abroad. This favorable view was largely confined to the early years of the Kennedy administration when the agency was new and its program for helping economic development overseas exerted a strong appeal among young people who had not yet found an equally appealing vocation in the war on poverty or environmental pollution at home.

More characteristically, the non-military sector of the foreign affairs bureaucracy has been on the defensive before the bar of public opinion, confronted with a deficit of public support rather than the surplus which the military ordinarily enjoys. Over virtually the entire period of the Cold War the State Department had been in a precarious position with respect to its public image, as has the U.S. Information Agency (USIA) and the various agencies charged with the conduct of foreign aid programs. In contrast to the Pentagon, the USIA is specifically prohibited by law from engaging in domestic propaganda activity. The efforts of these organizations in the field of public opinion formation have been largely defensive in character—designed to ward off attacks from critics of their activities. Congressional opponents of these agencies could find easy resonance for their attacks in attitudes of the public at large.

In carrying on their efforts to influence public attitudes, executive agencies in the field of foreign affairs are assisted by the fact that the public must rely on the government as a source of information to a much greater extent in international politics than it does on domestic issues. In most areas of domestic policy it is not hard to find private organizations which control as much if not more information than the government. In foreign affairs, on the other hand, there are many issues on which the bureaucratic apparatus stands virtually alone as a source of intelligence. By withholding certain kinds of data over which they have control, or on occasion by manufacturing and distributing false information, executive agencies can in fact lead the public to form wholly erroneous impressions of events taking place outside the United States. To be sure the deception of the American public may be unintentional. The primary purpose of releasing false information may be to mislead a foreign adversary. But in view of what we now know of what occurred in the Gulf of Tonkin in the summer of 1964, it is clear that the public was grossly misled by the information released by government agencies at that time—information that was subsequently used to justify and win public support for the full-scale American involvement in the Vietnam War.

For bureaucratic communications to reach the public, they must be transmitted through the facilities of the private media of communication. In this respect the media serve as instruments of bureaucratic power since they operate the principal channels through which the government can mobilize and manipulate public attitudes. Indeed, from the point of view of many executive officials, the proper role of the media in foreign affairs is to provide the government with just such an avenue through which it can transmit messages to the public. As one official put it, "Without strong, articulate information media, the Government cannot communicate with the electorate, or win popular support for the needs of national security."[11]

From the perspective of executive agencies, the chief asset of the media is the size of the audience they command. An agency's own publications reach only the comparatively small public which takes a continuing interest in its work. It is only through the privately owned and operated news media that the executive apparatus can reach mass opinion. Moreover, bureaucratic organizations have the capacity to induce the private media to give favorable coverage to their activities. By granting or withholding access to information or other favors coveted by reporters, they can inflict penalties upon journalists who write unfavorable stories, and provide rewards for those whose reports reflect official perspectives.[12] In the case of radio and television stations, the inducements are even more substantial, since these news outlets depend upon government licenses for their continued operation.

The Vietnam case in particular reveals that the media can impose a tremendously effective check upon the ability of executive agencies to manipulate mass opinion. Throughout the history of the war, reporters on the scene provided the public with alternative sources of information on the events taking place which conflicted with and on frequent occasions proved more accurate than the data made available by the government. In addition, the media

[11] Maxwell D. Taylor, "The War: The Record and the U.S.," *New York Times,* June 23, 1971, p. 43.

[12] For a recent examination of the power of executive agencies in this respect, see John Rothchild, "The Stories Reporters Don't Write," *Washington Monthly* 3 (June 1971): 20–27.

frequently exposed information in the possession of the executive branch that it would itself have preferred to conceal. Thus, while the media's claim to being a "fourth branch of government" may be exaggerated as far as some areas of domestic policy are concerned, it is certainly accurate for the sphere of foreign affairs.

Indeed, in the Vietnam War the media have been a far more troublesome adversary for the executive branch than Congress itself. Witness, for example, the fact that data which the executive was unwilling to turn over to the legislative branch was finally released to the public through the publication by the *New York Times* of the "Pentagon papers" in 1971. Hence it is not surprising that there has been so much antagonism toward the press and the other news media on the part of executive officials in recent years. Attacks on the media as a reliable source of information were common during the tenure of both Presidents Kennedy and Johnson, but they reached a peak during the early years of the Nixon administration. This was especially the case during the invasion of Laos in 1971, when adverse reports on the performance of South Vietnamese troops incensed the Defense Department, which was itself trying to persuade the public that the Laotian campaign had been a substantial if not a stunning success.

Whatever their other effects, these attacks testify to a recognition on the part of the executive branch of the power of the news media to shape public opinion on foreign affairs. Since this power threatens its own hegemony in the foreign policy process, the executive branch has responded to this challenge in recent years by seeking to undermine the standing of the news media in the public eye, charging the television networks in particular with bias and distortion in their coverage of the news. The accusation parallels and has presumably been designed to offset the charge of a "credibility gap" that has been so frequently leveled against executive officials themselves.

The credibility problem that executive officials encountered in Vietnam was a striking departure from the previous record of American foreign policy in the period since World War II. Although there were episodes in the Cold War prior to Vietnam in which questions were raised about the accuracy of official government announcements, there was no prior occasion on which the truthfulness of executive agencies was so frequently challenged, not only by the news media, but also by congressmen and a variety of private citizens and organizations.

In light of the Vietnam experience, it could be argued that the credibility of executive communications has been permanently impaired, and that as one of the many unanticipated consequences of the Vietnam War, the ability of bureaucratic organizations to shape opinion will never again be as great as it was in the first two decades of the Cold War. There is some evidence supporting this hypothesis, including public opinion polls which reveal growing public distrust of arguments advanced by the executive branch in support of the military action it has taken in Southeast Asia. But given the enduring sources of bureaucratic control over the communications process in foreign affairs, Vietnam may yet prove to have only transient effects in diluting the power of executive organizations to manipulate public opinion.

What the Vietnam case does more clearly reveal is the extent to which adversity in foreign affairs causes executive organizations to shift the target of their efforts to mold opinion from political elites to the masses. On most issues of foreign policy, mass opinion is quiescent. Major decisions are made in areas or about issues in which the mass public has virtually no interest at all. For example, in recent years the Strategic Arms Limitation Talks (SALT) on disarmament between the United States and the Soviet Union have been regarded by high government officials as being of critical importance for the development of national security policy in this country. Yet they have been carried on in an atmosphere of comparative invisibility as far as the general public is concerned. In this not unusual context of general public apathy, the opinion-forming activities of executive agencies tend to be directed toward so-called attentive publics—groups which take a continuing and quite intense interest in issues of foreign policy.

However, in the case of Vietnam there was widespread attrition in the support normally given American foreign policy by "attentive publics." The consensus that had held together throughout much of the Cold War suddenly came apart, and major elements of the press, the universities, and Congress became severely critical of American policy in Southeast Asia. In the face of this defection, there was an intensification of governmental efforts to win support for Vietnam policy from the public at large. After the Nixon administration took office in 1969, executive officials made a strong effort to compensate for loss of support for Vietnam policy within what might be called the foreign policy establishment in American society by appealing to the "silent majority" or "middle America" to sustain their country's foreign policy.

In carrying on their efforts to influence public opinion, executive organizations in the field of foreign affairs as in other areas of policy are restricted by law from direct involvement in propaganda or public relations activity. However, these laws readily lend themselves to evasion, since all administrative agencies are also charged with responsibility for keeping the public informed on what they are doing, and the line between unlawful propaganda and legitimate public information activity is as fine as any distinction that exists in the American political system.

Nevertheless, the presence of these legal barriers against propaganda activity by executive officials does create an incentive for bureaucratic organizations to use intermediaries in attempting to shape public opinion. Thus, agencies will often disclose information to a sympathetic congressman and rely on him to perform the task of disseminating it to the public at large. The transmission of information in this way represents a profitable exchange for both parties. The congressman attracts public attention to himself and enhances his own career by generating news. The executive organization gets its message across to the public and in the process ties a congressional supporter even more firmly to its own cause, since he has benefited from his role as intermediary for the organization. Members of the Armed Services Committee in both the House and Senate have often served their own and the Pentagon's purposes in precisely this fashion.

38

A friendly news media representative can perform the same function. An agency can "leak" information to a reporter or allow him to identify it as coming from "anonymous" or "highly placed" sources in the agency. Again the transaction is one that serves the interests of both the giver and the receiver of information. The agency succeeds in getting information disseminated to the public and the reporter or columnist obtains a highly prized exclusive story. Such relationships between the Pentagon and friendly newspaper columnists are not uncommon.

At the heart of the ability of bureaucratic organizations to form such exchange relationships for the dissemination of information is the classification system which shields information in the field of national security affairs from unauthorized disclosure to the public. The "top-secret," "secret," and "confidential" labels attached to documents whose secrecy is considered essential to national security do not prevent executive officials from releasing information contained in these documents when it serves their purposes to do so. While designed to prevent the release of information which would be damaging to the United States or its allies, or helpful to its adversaries abroad, the classification system also operates so as to assist the foreign affairs bureaucracies in manipulating public opinion. It enables them to conceal information that might reveal flows in their performance, while permitting the release of intelligence data that may strengthen their organizational position, as, for example, when disclosing information on an alleged improvement in Soviet weaponry may stimulate public support for increased appropriations for the Defense Department. Next perhaps to the defense contracts which the Pentagon is able to allocate within the domestic economy, no asset is more important to the continued power of the defense establishment than its ability to withhold or release information under the classification system.

III. THE CAPABILITIES OF BUREAUCRACY

Along with their ability to structure attitudes toward foreign policy issues, executive organizations also control the capabilities through which policy is carried out and upon which its success eventually depends. While elected officials may have grand designs in international politics, it is the determination and skill of the bureaucratic apparatus which frequently determine whether these objectives will be realized. In many situations the policy alternatives open to these officials are confined to the courses of action their organizational machinery has the will and the means to carry out. Bureaucratic resistance or incapacity may spell the doom of even the most modest policy proposals.

To no one is this kind of bureaucratic power of more critical importance than the president. There are many ways in which the executive apparatus over which he presides is an annoying burden to the chief executive. It often drags its feet in carrying out his proposals and frequently generates jurisdictional disputes he must settle—in this way consuming his time and exhausting his energy. But in the end the president is heavily dependent upon the ability of bureaucratic organizations for his own success. True, some of his policies may be largely self-executing. The decision of President Nixon in 1971 to turn American foreign policy away from its tradition of hostility toward Communist China is a notable example. But all too often, as in the case of President Johnson's consuming desire to "nail the coon-skin" of North Vietnam to his wall, the president's orders may be disastrous for him if their execution is beyond the capabilities of his bureaucracy.

Limiting Policy Options

The fact that bureaucratic organizations must perform the tasks necessary for the execution of policy is thus a major source of their influence over presidential decisions. Graham Allison has given us an illuminating description of the degree to which the choices of political leaders are limited by the talents of the bureaucratic organizations under their jurisdiction. As Allison puts it:

> . . . existing organizational routines for employing present physical capabilities constitute the range of effective choice open to government leaders confronted with any problem. . . . The fact that fixed programs (equipment, men, and routines that exist at the particular time) exhaust the range of buttons that leaders can push is not always perceived by these leaders. But in every case it is critical for an understanding of what is actually done.[1]

A telling illustration of Allison's argument was the role played by the development of a counter-insurgency capability in recent American foreign policy. During the 1950s one of the chief complaints leveled against the Eisenhower administration by such critics as Henry Kissinger was the fact that it lacked the organizational capacity to conduct small-scale, limited wars. Because of this deficiency, it was argued, policy-makers were forced to threaten nuclear war in situations in which it was not realistic to expect other countries to believe that this threat

[1] Graham T. Allison, *Essence of Decision: Explaining the Cuban Missile Crisis* (Boston: Little, Brown and Co., 1971), p. 79.

would ever be carried out. This weakness in its military arsenal deprived American foreign policy of much of its capacity to deter undesired behavior on the part of adversaries in international politics.

When John Kennedy was elected president in 1960, one of the primary items on his agenda was the creation of a limited war capability that would end the nation's exclusive and ineffective reliance upon the nuclear deterrent and enable it to cope with Communist-led guerrilla movements in the under-developed nations. The creation of this limited war capability under Kennedy made it possible for President Johnson to choose in 1965 to have American forces become directly and massively involved in ground combat in South Vietnam. In 1954, at an earlier stage of the war in Indo-China, when the United States had not yet developed such counter-insurgency techniques, President Eisenhower had declined to permit direct American participation in the war.

This is not to suggest that there is an iron law in national security affairs dictating that a bureaucratic capability once established will inevitably be used. In the past nations have acquired weapons they were unable to use in actual combat. For example, none of the participants in World War II used the chemical warfare resources at their disposal. This illustration reveals that a capability is unlikely to be employed if its use risks bringing costly retaliation in its wake.

It is also clear, however, that certain consequences do usually follow when a bureaucratic organization is created to provide foreign policy with a desired capability. For one thing such an organization will inevitably have a vested interest in its own survival. It will thus need to search for missions in which its value to society can be demonstrated and the flow of resources into the organization encouraged. Inevitably, it becomes a staunch protagonist of policies which enable it to display its skills, and these policies acquire a weight in executive deliberations they would not otherwise possess.

Hindsight suggests that the decision made in 1945 to drop atomic bombs upon the Japanese cites of Hiroshima and Nagasaki came largely from the fact that two major bureaucratic organizations which had a vested interest in using the bomb played an important role in determining that it would be employed—notwithstanding the fact that there were alternative policies available which might also have produced a Japanese surrender. One of these organizations was the Manhattan Project, which had built the bomb at what was then an enormous expense to the American taxpayer. From the point of view of the Manhattan organization, the use of the bomb in actual warfare was a tangible return for the labor it had expended and a demonstration to the public that its investment in the project had been worthwhile.

For a second organization, the air force, the dropping of the bomb was no such culminating achievement. The air force had already performed many other roles and missions in a war in which it had been engaged for almost four years. The use of this weapon was rather a means of taking out insurance on its future viability as an organizational component of the armed forces. Of the air force leaders chiefly involved in the decision to drop the bomb, one observer has commented:

Generals Arnold and Spaatz were both dedicated Air Force officers and hence had a distinctly Air Force perspective. In a war otherwise dominated by the Navy (including Naval Aviation), Arnold and Spaatz were naturally concerned with ensuring the fullest possible role for the Air Force in the defeat of Japan, and quick, effective use of atomic weapons would obviously bolster the service that delivered them—the Air Force. As Arnold put it: "The influence of atomic energy on Air Power could be stated very simply. It had made Air Power all-important." Thus the entire chain of command below Truman was populated by officials with a strong interest in seeing that the bomb, rather than some other measure, was used to end the war.[2]

Among the other measures available, for which there were no strong organizational protagonists, were a clarification of the terms of Japanese surrender—preserving the role of the emperor in Japanese society—, or a policy of waiting to assess the impact that Russian entrance into the Pacific war would have upon the Japanese will to resist.

The conclusion to which illustrations of this sort point is that a policy option which has a strong organizational advocate is much more likely to be adopted than one which lacks such sponsorship. Hence, predicting which of several possible policies will be followed in the conduct of foreign affairs can in no small measure be based on an assessment of the relative strength of the organizations responsible

[2] Kenneth M. Glazier, Jr., "The Decision to Use Atomic Weapons against Hiroshima and Nagasaki," *Public Policy* 18 (Summer 1970): 500.

for carrying out each of the options under consideration. Policy-makers will always be under strong pressure to follow courses of action that serve strong organizational interests and to ignore those that do not. For it needs always to be remembered that national security decisions are shaped primarily by the lobbying activity and pressures exerted by executive organizations rather than—as is commonly the case in domestic affairs—by private groups.[3]

In the making of foreign policy, organizations with highly technical capabilities have an advantage over those that lack such technical skills. The expertise of the Treasury Department is a case in point, since the influence of the department over presidential decisions on international trade and monetary policy is perhaps as formidable as that exercised by any executive agency in foreign affairs. For many presidents the whole subject of monetary policy is likely to be a source of bafflement, an area in which they must rely heavily upon the capabilities of their bureaucratic apparatus.

The State Department, on the other hand, has always had as a major disadvantage the fact that the thing it does best—diplomacy—is something the president is also likely to conceive he has a talent for. He may well regard diplomacy as an application of international problems of skills he has acquired in domestic politics—bargaining, dissembling, persuading and the other rudiments of the politician's art. While the president's domestic talents may not transfer as readily to the international arena as he imagines, the State Department is unlikely to increase

[3] See, in this connection, Samuel P. Huntington, *The Common Defense* (New York: Columbia University Press, 1961), p. 147.

the scope of its organizational authority by telling him so.

The most pathological possibility presented by the ability of bureaucratic organizations to define the options open to policy-makers is that organizational interests will come in time to transcend national interests, and that executive agencies will force the adoption of policies which reflect, not the needs and interests of the country, but their own appetite for power, prestige, or security. The best defense against this pathology is the existence of a variety of executive agencies with overlapping jurisdiction in the sphere of foreign affairs, or what has been called organizational "redundancy".[4] Where such pluralism prevails, organizations that become too introverted in their perspective risk losing out in the struggle for power to agencies that address themselves in a responsive way to national needs and problems as seen by the president, Congress, or the public. Allowing agencies to acquire a monopoly in the performance of a foreign policy function heightens the danger that organizational interests will become confused with national interests in the conduct of foreign affairs.

A most revealing illustration of the disparity between national and organizational interests in the administration of foreign policy is the extent to which organizations performing similar roles in two adversary nations help each other achieve their goals. The military bureaucracies in the United States and the Soviet Union have, in effect, been allied with

[4] Martin Landau, "Redundancy, Rationality, and the Problem of Duplication and Overlap," *Public Administration Review* 29 (July/August 1969): 346–58.

each other during the Cold War in the pursuit of complementary objectives, since the strength and development of the armed forces in each of the two countries have depended upon the health and vitality of the counterpart organization in the other.

The same is true of space agencies in the two countries, for whom the "space race" has been highly functional in terms of the financial support they have received from the public treasury. In a situation of such competitive interdependence between organizations in two hostile nations, it is useful for each of the agencies involved to heap praise upon the performance and efficiency of the other, since its own continued support depends upon the other's apparent effectiveness. It is not, therefore, surprising that U.S. space officials have so consistently praised the achievements of their organizational competitors in the Soviet bureaucracy. Anything less than lavish praise on their part would be clearly against their own organizational interests.

Executing Policy Decisions

Besides providing capabilities which in many cases define the options open to American foreign policy, bureaucratic organizations are also the instruments through which whatever policy is chosen will eventually be carried out. Few policy decisions made by the president or the National Security Council automatically translate themselves into the desired outcomes. The translation of decisions into results usually occurs as the end-product of the efforts of one or more bureaucratic organizations. The fact that decisions thus depend upon executive agencies for their implementation means that policy outcomes reflect, not only the intentions of the decision-makers, but also the characteristics of the organizations through which they are carried out. As a result, policy outputs generate many surprises among political officials responsible for decisions, or what organization theorists call "unanticipated consequences." In extreme cases the original intentions of policy-makers may hardly be visible in the outputs of the organization charged with putting decisions into effect.

Several characteristics of organizations help account for this tendency of organizational outcomes to differ from original policy decisions. It is common for executive agencies to execute decisions through what organization manuals describe as standard operating procedures—predetermined ways of handling specific problems as they arise. These routines are the set procedures through which an organization has carried out its responsibilities in the past, and they have been sanctified by tradition and usually by successful experience. Employees have been programmed to perform these procedures and they are often subject to sanctions if they deviate from them.

The ironic fact about such bureaucratic routines is that they are developed essentially to curb the ability of individual bureaucrats to influence policy through the exercise of personal discretion. Routines are designed to make the behavior of employees conform to organizational goals rather than their own personal inclinations. Organizations without routines place policy at the mercy of individual idiosyncrasies. But while intended to limit the power of executive officials, such routines may also have the effect of enormously increasing the power of bureaucratic organizations in the total governmental process.

Two characteristics of bureaucratic routines give them their special power—they are very difficult to start and, once begun, no less difficult to stop. Thus the celebrated law of bureaucratic inertia: "bureaucracies at rest tend to stay at rest, and bureaucracies in motion tend to stay in motion." The slowness with which bureaucratic organizations respond to presidential desires for action is legendary and a constant source of exasperation for chief executives. It was not until six weeks after President Kennedy's Vienna meeting with Khrushchev that the State Department finally prepared a response to the Russian leader's *aide mémoire* on Berlin.

> Kennedy had expected a quick American response capable, among other things, of making some appeal to world opinion. Instead, week followed week with no word from the Department, and the President's exasperation grew. When a draft finally came over in mid-July, nearly six weeks after Vienna, it was a tired and turgid rehash of documents left over from the Berlin crisis of 1958–59. . . . By this time it was too late to do anything but put the paper out. . . .[5]

Similarly, at the time of the Cuban missile crisis in October of 1962, Kennedy discovered that the American missiles he had ordered removed from Turkey several months earlier were still in place— a highly vulnerable target for Soviet efforts to win

---

[5] Arthur M. Schlesinger, Jr., *A Thousand Days* (Boston: Houghton Mifflin Co., 1965), p. 384.

American concessions in exchange for removing Russian missiles from Cuba.

> The President believed he was President and that, his wishes having been made clear, they would be followed and the missiles removed. He therefore dismissed the matter from his mind. Now he learned that his failure to follow up on this matter had permitted the same obsolete Turkish missiles to become hostages of the Soviet Union.[6]

The missiles were still in Turkey in October of 1962 because the State Department followed its normal procedure of international consultation before taking action. The Turks objected to the proposal when it was first presented to them, and the State Department was engaged in the patient (and often interminable) processes of diplomatic persuasion at the time the Cuban missile crisis erupted. The earlier indication by the president that he wished to have American missiles removed from Turkey had been a signal to the department to begin the lengthy processes of diplomacy necessary to accomplish this objective, not an order to by-pass these standard operating procedures in dealing with a nation tied closely to the United States through the North Atlantic Treaty Organization. From the department's point of view, the president had not meant his order to be carried out at the expense of alienating an invaluable ally.

Exasperating as the inertia of bureaucratic organizations often is for American presidents, it is not

[6] Robert F. Kennedy, *Thirteen Days: A Memoir of the Cuban Missile Crisis* (New York: New American Library, Inc., 1969), p. 95.

altogether without value to them. In 1969 an American reconnaissance plane was shot down by North Korea, and it was President Nixon's first inclination to launch a retaliatory air strike against North Korean airfields. He could not do so immediately, however, since it took considerable time for the American military apparatus to deploy the forces necessary to conduct such a mission. As it turned out, this delay provided Nixon with an opportunity to change his mind. "As the military slowly moved air and sea reinforcements toward Korea, his anger cooled and he decided against retaliatory raids."[7] The cumbersome routines through which bureaucratic organizations operate may thus save political officials from making an overly rapid or rash response in an emerging crisis.

If the slowness with which executive agencies act in emergency situations can be described as a function of the inertia which characterizes large organizations, the difficulty of stopping bureaucratic organizations once they are launched upon a course of action reflects the momentum which bureaucratic routines acquire after being initiated. This momentum may take the form of carrying on procedures no longer needed simply because they have been built into an organization's repertoire, and their discontinuance would bring a reduction in the scope of an agency's activities or perhaps require the release of personnel. It may also reflect the fact that bureaucratic services generate constituencies which oppose their liquidation.

In 1970, for example, it was discovered that the

[7] *New York Times,* Jan. 21, 1971, p. 12.

army was still carrying on surveillance over civilian political activities that had been started during the period of civil disorders some years earlier to help the army subdue riots in several American cities. Once they were begun, these procedures proved very difficult to stop, mainly because other agencies of the government came to depend upon military intelligence for information on suspected subversives. "The intelligence operation generated a demand for its product from the Justice Department, the FBI, police departments and other government agencies. A source close to the operation said, 'We created addicts for this stuff all over the Government.' " [8]

Bureaucratic momentum may thus manifest itself in the on-going performance of routines that are no longer required, since the problem to which they were addressed no longer exists. More critically, perhaps, such momentum may take the form of a series of logically progressive short-term decisions which escalate into consequences far beyond those originally intended. Some observers have interpreted the American involvement in Vietnam in precisely this way, as the final product of a series of continuing steps by bureaucratic organizations that were never intended to lead, as they ultimately did, into a major conflict. For example, the commitment of the air force to Vietnam led inescapably to the assignment of ground combat forces to protect the air bases that then became necessary, and the activities of such ground forces inevitably escalated from a simply protective role to "search and destroy" activities against the enemy to forestall enemy attacks upon these bases.

[8] *Ibid.,* Jan. 18, 1971, p. 22.

The tendency of bureaucratic momentum to transform small-scale commitments into large ones is highly visible in weapons development activities. Warner Schilling has shown that the original decision to enter upon the development of the hydrogen bomb was intended to leave open the possibility of discontinuing the project.[9] However, once the H-bomb project was started, it required such formidable investments of resources over long periods of time that policy-makers found themselves committed to the eventual production of the bomb as soon as they had decided to launch a preliminary inquiry to see if it was feasible to construct such a weapon.

This kind of bureaucratic momentum tends to invalidate the argument of Braybrooke and Lindblom that policy-making in the United States is protected from irrationality by the fact that it moves incrementally in one sequential step after another from initial decision to final outcome, thus permitting a discontinuance of effort or the reversal of direction at any point at which either is considered desirable.[10] In point of fact the momentum of the organizations charged with putting a decision into effect may make it very difficult to stop or reverse gears once the bureaucratic machinery has been set in motion. Irreversibility may thus become a major hazard of foreign policy decisions carried out through large organizations.

A major factor contributing to such irreversibility

[9] Warner Schilling, "The H-Bomb Decision: How to Decide without Actually Choosing," *Political Science Quarterly* 76 (March 1961): 24–46.

[10] David Braybrooke and Charles E. Lindblom, *A Strategy of Decision* (New York: Free Press of Glencoe, 1963).

is the fact that large bureaucracies arrive at policy positions only after an elaborate process of consultation and accommodation among diverse organizational interests. Agreements negotiated with such painstaking effort resist change, because such change would require reopening the whole bargaining process with no certainty that the trade-offs required might not yield a less effective policy outcome. Henry Kissinger puts it well in a perceptive essay on the role of bureaucracy in foreign affairs:

> . . . once the decision-making apparatus has disgorged a policy, it becomes very difficult to change it. The alternative to the status quo is the prospect of repeating the whole anguishing process of arriving at decisions. This explains to some extent the curious phenomenon that decisions taken with enormous doubt and perhaps with a close division become practically sacrosanct once adopted. The whole administrative machinery swings behind their implementation as if activity could still all doubts.[11]

A crucial aspect of diplomacy in a world in which foreign policy is conducted through large organizations is the fact that international agreements require elaborate negotiations within nations as well as between them. The participants in these internal negotiations are the large organizations charged with responsibility for foreign affairs. They must protect themselves from imperialist designs on their bureaucratic territory by organizational neighbors in their own country as well as by international adversaries.

[11] Henry A. Kissinger, *American Foreign Policy* (New York: W. W. Norton & Co., 1969), p. 20.

In Kissinger's words, "A form of administrative democracy results, in which a decision often reflects an attainable consensus rather than substantive conviction (or at least the two imperceptibly merge). The internal requirements of the bureaucracy may come to predominate over the purposes which it was intended to serve."[12]

The pathological effects that may occur when bureaucratic organizations are given responsibility for executing decisions has been an important factor generating the growing role of the White House staff in the foreign policy process, particularly the dominant part now played by the special assistant for national security affairs. The difficulty presidents have in monitoring and controlling decisions once they are turned over to the ordinary departmental organizations for enforcement has led inevitably to a preference for carrying out major international decisions through White House assistants who make up in loyalty and responsiveness to the president what they may lack in formal diplomatic experience.

This tendency has been particularly pronounced in the case of President Nixon, who differs from earlier presidents in that he looks at the ordinary bureaucratic apparatus in foreign affairs as not only subject to organizational pathologies which inhibit its effective performance but also as personally antagonistic to him. Nixon's fears on this score are not entirely a case of presidential paranoia. Leaks from the executive branch in both the Eisenhower and his own administration could well be interpreted as efforts to discredit White House policies. In 1958, during

12 *Ibid.*, pp. 20–21.

his tenure as vice-president, Nixon charged the State Department with "undercutting" and "sabotage" of official policy when it released a breakdown of mail from constituents which showed heavy public opposition to an American commitment to defend the islands of Quemoy and Matsu off the Chinese mainland.[13] In 1972 Nixon was confronted with another leak from the bureaucratic apparatus on secret American efforts to assist Pakistan during the period when the administration had publicly pledged itself to neutrality in the India-Pakistan war. Such leaks are perhaps a special source of annoyance to Nixon because they link executive officials in a hostile conspiracy with the media of communication, and throughout his political life Nixon has been even more suspicious of reporters than of bureaucrats.

Hence the notion of presidential dominance of foreign affairs as argued by Wildavsky among others needs to be qualified somewhat.[14] Such dominance has been quite striking since World War II if attention is centered on the president's struggles with Congress in major policy disputes, since the legislature has commonly deferred to the chief executive on foreign policy issues. Letting the president have his way in international affairs is the path of elementary political prudence for Congress, since the sixth political sense of legislators tells them that the president can easily monopolize all political credit for achievements in foreign affairs, but, by failing to

[13] See MacAlister Brown, "The Demise of State Department Public Opinion Polls: A Study in Legislative Oversight," *Midwest Journal of Political Science* 5 (February 1961): 16.

[14] Aaron Wildavsky, "The Two Presidencies," *Trans-Action* 4 (December 1966): 7–14.

follow his lead, they risk sharing the blame for any failures that may occur. But the picture changes somewhat if attention is shifted from the president's relations with Congress to his relations with the ordinary executive apparatus. In this area, as the preceding discussion has shown, the president can easily meet frustration and defeat in his desire to see his policies carried out.

One keen observer of presidential politics, Richard Neustadt, argues that it is the bluntness of large organizations which makes them ineffective as instruments for the realization of policy objectives.

> Our contemporary "big" bureaucracy in national security affairs, so-called, is a blunt instrument. On the record of the past it is effectively responsive to blunt challenges when gripped by a blunt policy. Its character was shaped in World War and in Cold War. Yet the era of such challenges seems to be behind us. Blunt policy no longer serves. Subtlety, however, is a thing for which this instrument was not designed, with which I have my doubts it can learn to cope.[15]

Much the same argument has been made by Paarlberg with respect to the role of bureaucratic organizations in foreign affairs: "Initiatives, once taken, must be followed through with imagination and flexibility, and the bureaucracy has neither."[16]

In trying to carry out foreign policy through the regular executive departments, nothing is more irri-

---

[15] Richard E. Neustadt, *Alliance Politics* (New York: Columbia University Press, 1970), pp. 148–49.

[16] Rob Paarlberg, "The Domestication of American Foreign Policy," *Public Policy* 18 (Winter 1970): 258.

tating to presidents than the fact that there are so
many nooks and crannies through which information
can leak to the outside world. President Johnson
regarded this as a major disadvantage in conducting
the Vietnam War. In his memoirs he complains
bitterly of the unauthorized release of information
by executive officials at the time of the Tet offensive
in 1968 disclosing General Westmoreland's request
for additional reinforcements for the American
forces then under seige by the North Vietnamese.
President Nixon has reduced the possibility of such
leaks by centering responsibility in the White House
staff for the execution of major foreign policy initiatives—such as the rapprochement with China in
1971. If secrecy is a requirement of effective diplomacy, as is widely believed to be the case, then a
major problem of trying to execute decisions through
large bureaucratic organizations is the fact that, as
has often been charged, they "leak like a sieve."

Of course outsiders may look upon the unauthorized release of classified information, not as a form
of bureaucratic pathology, but as a check upon mind-
less momentum in executive policy-making. Before
the disclosure of Westmoreland's request for additional troops, American policy in Vietnam had moved
steadily upward along a path of continuing escalation
in the apparent pursuit of military victory. After
public exposure of the Westmoreland proposal, the
policy of escalation was halted, and the Johnson
administration made proposals to the North Vietnamese which led eventually to the beginning of negotiations in Paris and to a reduction of the American
presence in Vietnam. Thus what may appear as a
pathological characteristic of large-scale bureaucracy

from the president's perspective—the fact that it can't keep secrets—may be regarded as a healthy attribute by members of the public who are opposed to administration policy, or interested in making foreign policy responsive to public opinion.

Of all the factors that give bureaucracy power over the execution of decisions, none perhaps is more important than the simple ability of executive agencies to do nothing. Inertia has been termed the most potent form of bureaucratic energy, and its impact is writ large over the development of American foreign policy in recent years. A study of the way in which the United States became inadvertently committed to the defense of the islands held by the Chinese Nationalists off the mainland of China concludes that it constitutes a "sobering example in the realm of foreign policy of the general proposition that to make the bureaucracy change its position is much more difficult than allowing it to continue a given policy: the bureaucracy prefers the known dangers of an existing course to the uncertain costs and gains of change."[17]

This kind of bureaucratic veto by inaction is akin to what has been described as nondecision-making—the ability of some participants in the policy process to prevent certain kinds of decisions from even appearing on the agenda of choice. Where bureaucratic influence of this sort prevails, executive organizations are certainly in a position to exclude some foreign policy alternatives from consideration in

[17] Morton Halperin and Tang Tsou, "United States Policy Toward the Offshore Islands," *Public Policy* 15 (Cambridge: Harvard University Press, 1966): 137.

policy discussions altogether.[18] The core of bureaucratic power becomes the ability not to make things happen but to prevent them from happening.

In pointing to the power represented by bureaucratic inertia, it is important to remember that resistance to change in foreign policy springs from other sources as well. Throughout the period following World War II American foreign policy was sustained by a political consensus that was quite inhospitable to new ideas, if they appeared to contravene in any way the principle of containing the expansion of Communist power. Bureaucratic rigidity may thus reflect bureaucratic pathology—the inability of executive agencies to adapt to change in the environment, or to alter organizational policies and procedures once they have become established. It may also mirror the influence of domestic political forces which executive organizations are fearful of offending. The rigidity of American policy toward China in the two decades following the rise of the Communists to power was in large part a function of just such political factors. When President Nixon decided in 1971 that the political barriers to détente with China were no longer insuperable, he was not seriously hindered in launching upon a new policy by bureaucratic inertia.

[18] For a discussion of nondecision-making as a form of power see Peter Bachrach and Morton S. Baratz, *Power and Poverty* (New York: Oxford University Press, 1970), pp. 39–51.

IV. BUREAUCRATIC PATHOLOGY AND FOREIGN AFFAIRS

This discussion has pursued what may well seem to be contradictory objectives. On the one hand it has emphasized the substantial role that bureaucratic organizations now play in the foreign policy process, and traced the paths through which their influence affects decisions in international affairs. At the same time it has stressed the fact that this power is exercised in the United States within the framework of a political system that sets limits, however shifting or imprecise, upon its scope.

Two avenues of bureaucratic power have been identified as having special importance. One is the ability of executive agencies to shape the views of elected officials and the general public on foreign policy issues. The other is the fact that bureaucratic organizations have technical capabilities upon which the achievement of policy goals often depends. Joined together in the same organization, the cumulative power represented by these resources is formidable, and on many issues it is sufficient to enable bureaucratic organizations to determine the direction of policy.

The salient role played by bureaucratic organizations in the evolution of recent American foreign policy is clear. Without extraordinary bureaucratic capabilities, it would not have been possible to build and deploy atomic weapons during and after World War II—a development which has had a profound effect upon the character of American foreign policy in the postwar years. During the same period disarmament negotiations with the Soviet Union have been shaped by the technical knowledge and advice of the Atomic Energy Commission, and in years to come such negotiations will continue to be profoundly affected by the expertise of science, intelligence and defense agencies.

However dominant they may sometimes seem to be in the international area, bureaucratic organizations are only part of the political system in any democratic political order. Their advice may have compelling force in policy deliberations, particularly when it is coupled with predictions of the dire consequences that will ensue if their suggestions are not taken. But the plain fact of the matter is that on many important issues since World War II, the advice of even the most powerful of national security organizations—the military—has not had a controlling effect. As Arthur Schlesinger has written:

> At best, all those who give advice can do is give it, but the decisions are made by—and the responsibility rests on—those who take the advice. . . . Essentially, it is the acceptance on the part of the President and the Secretary of State of such advice that makes it significant rather than the fact that elements of the bureaucracy generate it.[1]

The same kind of limitation surrounds bureaucratic capabilities. However impressive these capabilities may be as instruments of policy, there is no iron law which dictates that they will in fact be used. Indeed, from the perspective of many bureaucratic organizations, the most striking thing about their

[1] In Richard M. Pfeffer, ed., *No More Vietnams* (New York: Harper & Row, 1968), pp. 85–86.

own skills is the fact that they are so seldom employed, or when used, are subject to such stringent political constraints. This has certainly been the view of the armed forces with respect to the restricted use of American military capacities in Vietnam. During the Nixon administration foreign service officers in the State Department have resented the fact that their expertise has been so largely ignored by the president.

What these illustrations suggest is that bureaucratic organizations are linked in a policy system in which they sometimes play a secondary part. The other participants—outside groups, Congress, and most especially the president and the White House staff—can at times reduce bureaucrats to a very subordinate status in policy deliberations. Indeed, the task of divining and conforming to presidential prejudices and preferences is a common bureaucratic preoccupation in Washington.

Many bureaucrats would ruefully contend that their influence is largely restricted to the disposition of run-of-the-mill matters in foreign affairs. Once an issue becomes important, the president or Congress move in and seize jurisdiction or greatly reduce the scope of bureaucratic control over it. At the time of the Cuban missile crisis, for example, the ordinary executive agencies engaged in the administration of foreign affairs were almost totally excluded from policy deliberations as the president and the executive committee of the national security council met to hammer out tactics of confrontation with the Soviet Union. The same thing happened when international monetary and trade issues became critical in 1971.

The amount of power that bureaucratic organizations actually exert over foreign policy decisions thus depends, not only upon their own resources for extending their influence, but also upon the passivity of other participants in the policy process. When public opinion is aroused, as in the case of Vietnam, the authority of bureaucracy diminishes. When Congress or the president are inattentive to foreign policy issues, because of their preoccupation with domestic questions or for other reasons, the influence of bureaucracy grows apace. Bureaucratic power is thus the greatest on matters of routine in the area of foreign policy. It is the least in a period of crisis.

Reforming the Bureaucracy

Control over what other participants in the foreign policy process may perceive as matters of routine still gives the bureaucratic apparatus jurisdiction over a very high proportion of day-to-day issues. The way in which executive agencies handle these routine responsibilities may well decide whether or not a crisis emerges or even predetermine its outcome. As one observer has noted in a criticism of recent efforts to centralize control over national security decisions in the hands of the president, foreign policy "grows out of day-to-day actions taken and commitments made by officials outside the White House."[2]

Since the success or failure of policy does so frequently turn on the routine work of executive agencies, the goal of improving the quality of bureaucratic performance in carrying on the tasks

[2] I. M. Destler, "Can One Man Do" *Foreign Policy* 5 (Winter 1971–72): 39.

of diplomacy will continue to be high on the agenda of administrative reform in the United States. In the past these efforts have sought mainly to overcome what Stanley Hoffmann calls the "splintering of the executive branch."[3] The concern of reformers has centered on the fact that foreign policy is carried on through a very large family of organizations in the United States, so that the country often seems to be pursuing not one but a variety of policies abroad. Moreover, some of the members of this organizational network in foreign affairs duplicate each other's activities, others seek to attain contradictory goals. (All commonly suffer from the bureaucratic maladies described in the previous chapter—rigidity in outlook, adherence to routine, and slowness to adapt to changing demands from the environment.)

The standard remedy for organizational overlapping and duplication has been to improve coordination among the diverse agencies playing a role in foreign affairs. Landmark steps in this direction include the unification of the armed forces and the establishment of the National Security Council. Since these developments seemed to many observers to give the Defense Department undue primacy in the national security apparatus, suggestions have repeatedly been made that the State Department be assigned a leading role in coordinating the programs of all executive agencies engaged in activities abroad.

However, since the Vietnam War there has been a dramatic change in perspective on the question of what constitutes organizational pathology in foreign affairs, for a trauma like Vietnam reveals many

[3] Stanley Hoffmann, *Gulliver's Troubles* (New York: McGraw-Hill Co., 1968), pp. 266–80.

bureaucratic weaknesses that would otherwise remain hidden from view. Suddenly, concern over the performance of executive agencies is no longer restricted to the way in which they coordinate their activities in the pursuit of agreed-upon objectives but it has begun to focus also upon the way in which these agencies decide upon their objectives. Thus efforts at organizational reform no longer put exclusive emphasis on the need to maximize the coherence of policy. In the wake of Vietnam, it has become equally vital to encourage dialogue and deliberation so as to prevent decisions from being reached before all options have been examined and before the costs and consequences of alternative policies have been thoroughly explored.

As a result there has been increasing interest in organizational arrangements that will promote not only coordination of activity but diversity of thought. In the view of many observers, the most damaging setback for American foreign policy since World War II—the Vietnam War—resulted in no small measure from the fact that agreement was reached before all alternatives were given adequate consideration. In this case consensus may have been premature precisely because it was too eagerly sought after. Such are the fruits of a Vietnam policy that now seems with hindsight to be the logical product of a national security system in which coordination was overly prized and dissent insufficiently appreciated. It is true, however, that it is very hard to invent structural arrangements that will enhance coordination and diversity at the same time. Measures designed to promote one of these goals usually retard achievement of the other.

Vietnam has also focused attention on the difficulties that beset efforts to attain policy goals once they are decided on. It has become increasingly evident that no policy decision should be finalized before the case or difficulty of carrying it out have been taken into account, at least where the use of large-scale organizational processes is essential for the achievement of program objectives. In the past, the appraisal of policy alternatives has not ordinarily included the feasibility of implementation within the framework of analysis. This is what Graham Allison calls the "analysis gap"—the failure to study the area lying "between preferred solutions and the actual behavior of the government." [4]

This new interest in implementation contrasts sharply with the attention that was lavished in the 1960s on improved techniques for deciding on courses of action—systems analysis, cost-effectiveness ratios and the other instruments of managerial science. It is now recognized that the most advanced techniques for making decisions are of little avail when the organizations needed to translate these decisions into results are either non-existent or ineffective.

Foreign Policy and the Palace Guard

Since the coming to power of the Nixon administration in 1969, it is only a small exaggeration to say that the cure for the ills of bureaucracy in handling major problems of international politics has been to dispense with it altogether—or, at least to do without that part of the bureaucracy represented by the ordinary executive agencies having tradi-

[4] Graham Allison, *Essence of Decision: Explaining the Cuban Missile Crisis* (Boston: Little, Brown and Co., 1971), p. 267.

tional responsibility for the conduct of foreign affairs. Upon taking office, President Nixon moved quickly to center decision-making power in the hands of the National Security Council staff under the direction of his own special assistant for national security affairs, Henry Kissinger.[5]

In the first days after its establishment in 1947, the National Security Council served mainly to ensure that all the principal agencies involved in foreign policy would participate in executive decision-making. The role of the special assistant was not primarily to advise the president but to make certain that he was exposed to the views of the executive organizations that had a legitimate right to be consulted before a decision was reached.

President Nixon brought to fulfillment a trend that had been clearly visible during the Kennedy and Johnson years. The special assistant for national security affairs now took on the chief advisory function and also monitored the communications channeled to the president from the regular executive establishment. By 1971 Kissinger was generally recognized as the president's chief deputy on all matters of salient importance in foreign affairs—by the public, by other participants in the foreign policy process, and even by the heads of foreign governments.

The growth of Kissinger's power in the Nixon administration reflects, to some extent, the impact

[5] For recent analyses of these Nixon innovations, see Destler, "Can One Man Do"; John P. Leacacos, "Kissinger's Apparat," *Foreign Policy* 5 (Winter, 1971–72): 3–27; and Alexander L. George, "The Case for Multiple Advocacy in Making Foreign Policy," paper prepared for delivery at the 1971 Annual Meeting of the American Political Science Association.

of personal style upon organizational structure. President Nixon had always questioned the loyalty of the national security bureaucracy to him, and it was not surprising that he chose to concentrate power over foreign policy in the White House rather than the State Department. Henry Kissinger's negative estimate of the capacity of large-scale organizations to operate effectively in international politics had already appeared in print when he assumed his duties as President Nixon's chief aide on foreign policy.[6]

But this concentration of power in the White House also mirrored the declining prestige of the regular bureaucratic apparatus in foreign affairs. Whatever judgments history may eventually make on responsibility for the Bay of Pigs and the Vietnam War, virtually all immediate postmortem examinations were highly critical of the role played by executive agencies and in many cases laid the chief responsibility for failure on their doorstep. Hence, when Nixon came to power, the time was ripe for organizational rearrangements which would reduce bureaucratic authority over the conduct of foreign policy.

It remains to be seen, however, if this effort to escape bureaucratic pathologies will not subject the foreign policy process to an equally serious set of vices associated with government by the palace guard. One traditional failing of bureaucratic decision-making, the fact that it often fails to reflect or anticipate public opinion, seems at least as much a deficiency of a foreign policy made exclusively

[6] Henry A. Kissinger, "Domestic Structure and Foreign Policy," *Daedalus* 95 (Spring, 1966): 503–29.

from the White House. The outbreak of violent protests and civil disorders that occurred in the wake of the decision to invade Cambodia in 1970 did not appear to have been anticipated by President Nixon or his White House staff. And again, when the administration aligned itself with Pakistan during the India-Pakistan war of 1971, the presidential circle seemed far out of touch with a public opinion that seemed to be either neutral or favorable toward India.

Indeed, it could be argued that foreign policy-making by a palace guard is even more insulated from public opinion than a process which includes the regular executive establishment within the circle of discussion. To be sure executive agencies are themselves characteristically insensitive to public opinion. But on balance their larger and more representative structure of membership certainly provides a more adequate pretest of probable public sentiment than is available when deliberations prior to decision are carried out entirely within the inner sanctum of the White House.

Moreover, in earlier discussion we have noted the tendency of executive agencies to leak information in their custody. This practice, disadvantageous as it may be for the president, does provide an opportunity for the public and Congress to learn about and to react to decisions before they are finalized. Such an opportunity is not as readily available when discussions are confined to the presidential office. As President Nixon demonstrated—most notably with respect to his announcement in 1971 of his forthcoming trip to Communist China—a chief executive can prevent leaks from his own staff much more easily than from the executive branch as a whole. While such secrecy helps a president achieve surprise, it also effectively excludes Congress and the public from any opportunity to influence policy before it is made.

It also seems clear that the strategy of centering control over foreign policy in the White House subjects it, to an undesirable extent, to the influence of White House personalities. Since World War II the prejudices and ambitions of American presidents have had a compelling impact upon the development of American foreign policy in ways that often seem every bit as pathological as the vices attributed to bureaucratic decision-making. Witness the influence at the time of the Cuban missile crisis in 1962 of Kennedy's feeling that he had been betrayed by Khrushchev. "He can't do this to me!" was Kennedy's initial response to the information that the Russians were placing missiles in Cuba. Or consider what has now become almost legendary in American politics—Johnson's fear in 1965 that he would suffer the disgrace of being the first American president to lose a war, or Nixon's desire at the time of the Cambodian invasions in 1970 to recoup prestige he had lost through a series of domestic defeats including the rejection of two Supreme Court nominees by the Senate.

This record is not presented in order to argue that major events in recent American foreign policy can be primarily explained as presidential "ego trips." What it does clearly indicate, however, is that if bureaucratic decision-making tends to be inordinately influenced by organizational ambitions, White House decision-making may suffer in equal measure from the pathology of personal ambition. Moreover, when decision-making in foreign affairs is monopolized by the president and his immediate entourage, the possibility that such personality factors will exert an unhealthy influence is greatly reinforced. As George Reedy has pointed out, the men around the president are accustomed to accept not to challenge his authority.[7] In both the Johnson and the Nixon administration, dissent has come primarily from the executive departments, not the White House staff, where, if Reedy is to be believed, sycophancy is a common failing.

Finally, it is questionable if the concentration of power over foreign affairs in the White House does anything to solve the major problem associated with decision-making by bureaucratic organizations—the failure to open up and explore all alternatives before making decisions. In broadening the authority of the special assistant over foreign policy, Nixon and Kissinger had the ostensible objective of widening the options of the president on the issues that came before him. Their fear was that the national security organizations in the executive branch would negotiate and compromise differences on issues and present the president with a united front in support or opposition to a projected course of action. In such situations, the president would be reduced to the role of ratifying not initiating foreign policy decisions. As President Nixon put it, "I refuse to be confronted with a bureaucratic consensus that leaves me no options but acceptance or rejection, and that

[7] George E. Reedy, *The Twilight of the Presidency* (New York: The World Publishing Co., 1970).

gives me no way of knowing what alternatives exist." [8]

The organizational remedy adopted to prevent the premature foreclosure of presidential choice— the centralization of decision-making in the office of the special assistant for national security affairs— hardly seems to escape the problem it was designed to solve. To be sure, the regular bureaucratic apparatus is now less able to suppress alternatives that should be brought to the president for his consideration, whether by negotiating a unified position through interorganizational bargaining, or by offering him several options of which only one could be taken seriously.

But executive centralization is at the opposite extreme from the organizational pluralism that has always been the chief source of diverse viewpoints in bureaucracy. Without a multitude of conflicting organizational interests and centers of power, it is difficult to see how the vigor and variety of dialogue and dissent at lower echelons can be sustained. Inevitably, the centering of so much authority in the office of the special assistant for national security affairs will have a depressing effect upon independence of thought and initiative at other levels of the system. What is clearly required is organizational strength at the bottom as well as the top, if executive deliberations are to retain any vitality.

Presidential and National Interests

Of course, what the Nixon-Kissinger innovations are mainly designed to do is insure the responsiveness

[8] George, "The Case for Multiple Advocacy in Making Foreign Policy," p. 3.

of the organizational machinery in foreign affairs to the president's control, so that decisions reflect the chief executive's wishes. Certainly, these new organizational arrangements help achieve that objective. There remains, however, a nagging question which the events of recent history make particularly acute. Is an arrangement that suits the president's interests equally useful for the country? Since Vietnam there has been doubt on this score, as evidence accumulates that the decisions of presidents on matters of foreign policy may mirror to an undesirable extent their own personality needs and deficiencies, or the imperatives of presidential politics. It has become increasingly clear that presidents and presidential aides frequently suffer from the same failing as bureaucratic organizations—the tendency to use foreign policy for self-aggrandizement and to pursue their own rather than the nation's interests abroad.

Hence, organizational structures for the conduct of foreign affairs need to be appraised in terms of the interests of the public as well as the president. From this perspective, executive organizations may be seen as providing a useful check upon the president in the arena of international politics—a check which is removed when excessive power is concentrated in the office of the special assistant for national security affairs. Thus, these organizations serve as a brake upon hasty action in foreign affairs, especially when such undue haste may reflect presidential emotion rather than rational calculation.

Moreover, because of a relatively independent position as organizations having their own professional traditions and outside constituencies, executive agencies subject the chief executive's proposals on foreign policy issues to much more searching scrutiny than they would normally receive from his own somewhat deferential and presidentially oriented staff. Particularly in a nation like the United States which lacks a collective institution like a cabinet which can restrain the president from unwise decisions on foreign affairs, executive organizations can be regarded as a useful element of balance in a system which in modern times has been all too prone to fall under absolute domination by the man in the White House.[9]

Undoubtedly, the failings of bureaucratic organizations in carrying on the administration of foreign affairs are many, as earlier discussion has clearly shown. But the best cure for these deficiencies will come from efforts both to revitalize the agencies in which they exist, and to make these organizations more responsive to public control, not the transfer of authority to a White House coterie that is susceptible to these same failings, and also prey to the diseases of court politics—insulation from the public, genuflection toward the throne, and an unhealthy preoccupation with the impact of international events upon the palace rather than the country.

This is not to suggest that the system President Nixon inaugurated of centralizing control over foreign policy decisions under the National Security Council staff is altogether without merit. Clearly,

[9] In the minds of some of its sponsors, one of the major purposes of the National Security Council, as originally constituted, was to provide just such a check upon the president from within the executive. See Paul Y. Hammond, "The National Security Council as a Device for Inter-Departmental Coordination: An Interpretation and Appraisal," *American Political Science Review* 54 (December 1960): 899–910.

this arrangement permits more timely decisions than are possible when a great many bureaucratic organizations must be consulted before an issue can be resolved. It thus prevents policy initiatives from being stymied by the obstructionism and foot-dragging that often characterize the behavior of executive agencies anxious to defend their own jurisdictional interests. In interagency forums like the National Security Council, bureaucracies have often attempted to suppress the discussion of issues or the presentation of information that they regard as disadvantageous to their own organizational ambitions.

Because it is so antibureaucratic in its thrust, the new system clearly responds to the hostility against the bureaucratic apparatus in foreign affairs spawned by the Vietnam War. The question we have raised here is whether some of this animus should not be more appropriately directed toward the presidential office, where much of the responsibility for following policies ill-suited to advance the security interests of the United States must ultimately be placed.

To many observers the lesson that Vietnam seems to teach is the necessity of opening up the foreign policy process to wider circles of participation. It is increasingly proposed that Congress be given an opportunity to share in major policy decisions before they are made, rather than having to accommodate to a *fait accompli* by the president as has so often been the case in the past. Suggestions have also been made that the public be provided with more effective channels through which it can convey its views on foreign affairs to agencies like the State Department. As far as the internal operation of the executive branch itself is concerned, the opportunity for such broad participation in foreign policy decisions is greatest under a decentralized system when many agencies provide access to executive deliberations. It is least under a tightly-knit, hierarchical system run by the White House.

In light of this background, the Nixon achievement in centering control over foreign policy in his own hands is a remarkable *tour de force* in contemporary American politics. Coming to power in 1969 at a time when the presidential office was perhaps at the point of its lowest esteem in American political life since 1932, with revisionist critics increasingly suggesting that the presidency was a source of evil as well as good in American life,[10] Nixon not only fended off attacks upon presidential primacy in foreign affairs but also moved to make the president's hegemony even more secure by adding the bureaucracy to Congress as institutions effectively excluded from a major role in the foreign policy process.

The argument used to justify this *coup* was that the president needed to have "options," and that the effect of bureaucratic participation in decision-making was to narrow the choices open to a chief executive. It is not perhaps excessive cynicism to suggest that the net effect of the new arrangement is not so much to widen the president's options on foreign policy as to increase his control over it and to diminish the influence of others.

It may well be asked why after highlighting the

[10] For an analysis of this revisionist critique of the presidency, see Thomas F. Cronin, "The Textbook Presidency and Political Science," paper prepared for delivery at the 66th Annual Meeting of the American Political Science Association, Sept. 7–12, 1970.

shortcomings of bureaucratic organizations throughout this analysis, we should return in the end to a defense of their role in foreign affairs. But the fact of the matter is that, if these organizations do not participate in decision-making, then the president for all practical purposes "corners the power-market."[11] In foreign affairs the system of checks and balances does not work as an arrangement under which Congress acts as a real counterweight to the president. The House is docile even submissive to the chief executive on issues of international politics, and the Senate, although considerably more independent, has not, by its own admission, been able to challenge the president effectively.

Thus, insofar as there are to be any checks upon the president's power over foreign affairs by governmental institutions, they must come through the interplay among executive organizations or between these organizations and the White House. It is only from the internal workings of the executive branch itself that the Federalist principle of institutional balance can realize itself in foreign policy. It is no cure for the effects of bureaucratic pathology on foreign affairs to exclude executive organizations, in addition to Congress and the public, from effective participation in decisions, thus giving the president sole power to decide how best to pursue American interests abroad. Such a monopoly, reminiscent of European "cabinet diplomacy" in the nineteenth

[11] This phrase is used by Marilyn Gittell to describe the role of the central supervisory staff in the New York city school system. See Marilyn Gittell, "Professionalism and Public Participation in Educational Policy-Making: New York City, A Case Study," *Public Administration Review* 27 (September 1967): 247.

century, greatly enhances the likelihood that the foreign policy of the United States will serve presidential rather than national interests. This is a continuing problem in election years, when presidents are under special temptation to generate events and crises from which they can draw political profit at home by a display of executive vigor abroad.

Library of Congress Cataloging in Publication Data

Rourke, Francis Edward, 1922-
  Bureaucracy and foreign policy.

  (Studies in international affairs, no. 17)
  Includes bibliographical references.
  1. United States—Executive departments.
  2. United States—Foreign relations administration.
  I. Title. II. Series: Washington Center of Foreign Policy
  Research. Studies in international affairs, no. 17.

JK421.R59   353.008'92   73-186516
ISBN 0-8108-1394-8
ISBN 0-8108-1399-9 (pbk.)